WELCO
POLI

MW00959200

LEARN ABOUT THE HISTORY OF...

Prehistoric Poland • Mieszko • Annexations • November Uprising • Great Emigration • January Uprising • World Wars 1 & 2 • Sanation Movement • Polish October • Radom massacre • Solidarity • Fall of Communism • Cold War • Table Talks • Polish Democracy • Warsaw Uprising • City of Krakow • Jasna Góra Monastery • Auschwitz-Birkenau • Wieliczka Salt Mine • Malbork Castle • Polin, Warsaw, & Czartoryski Museums • Pierogi • Bigos • Kielbasa • Zapiekanka • Rosol • Sernik • Paczki • Football • Volleyball • Track and Field • Skiing

ILLUSTRATED WITH HISTORICAL PHOTOS

THE HiSTORY OF POLAND...

The land that is modern-day Poland has been inhabited since the pre-historic stone age, and the peoples that have lived in Poland have had a large impact on our world ever since.

We will learn about what Poland was like during prehistoric times and find out about one of Poland's first rulers named **Mieszko**. Poland has faced many attacks by other nations during its history and the country was pieced up by annexations of neighboring countries. You'll discover the events of the World Wars, and how they shaped Poland's history. Poland faced numerous revolutions that would change the course of the country's history such as the January uprising, Sanation movement, Warsaw uprising, and Polish October. Some of the world's most fascinating locations are in Poland and we will visit the **Wieliczka Salt Mine, Malbork Castle,** and some of the beautiful national museums. Finally, you'll finish the journey of learning about Poland by discovering some delicious foods like Pierogi, and playing some of the country's most popular sports, like football.

Let's learn about the history of Poland.

EARLY POLISH HISTORY

The earliest evidence of human habitation in what is now Poland dates back to the Paleolithic era, around 500,000 years ago. The first permanent settlements, however, did not appear until the Neolithic era, around 6,000 BCE. These early communities were characterized by agriculture, pottery-making, and the development of simple tools and weapons.

Over time, these early Polish societies grew increasingly complex, developing trade networks, metallurgy, and social hierarchies. By the Bronze Age (around 2300-700 BCE), several distinct cultures had emerged in the region, including the Lusatian and Oksywie cultures. These societies were characterized by their use of bronze tools and weapons, as well as the practice of cremation and elaborate burial rituals.

During the Iron Age (around 700 BCE-400 CE), several powerful tribes and kingdoms emerged in the region. One of the most significant of these was the Pomeranian culture, which extended along the Baltic Sea coast and controlled a vast trade network that stretched as far as Scandinavia and the Black Sea. Other important tribes included the Przeworsk culture, which controlled the central part of present-day Poland, and the Biskupin culture, which built a large fortified settlement on a lake island near the modern city of Poznań.

The origins and rise of the Polish state can be

traced back to the 10th century, when a tribal leader named Mieszko I united several Slavic tribes and established a centralized monarchy in the region. Under Mieszko and his successors, the Polish state rapidly expanded, incorporating vast territories to the east and south.

During this period, Poland also became a major center of Christianity. In 966, Mieszko was baptized and declared Christianity the official religion of Poland. This move had important political and cultural implications, as it helped to integrate Poland into the wider Christian world and gave the Polish state greater legitimacy in the eyes of its neighbors.

Over the next several centuries, Poland continued to expand its territory and influence. In the 14th century, the Polish-Lithuanian Commonwealth was established, creating one of the largest and most powerful states in Europe. The Commonwealth was characterized by a unique political system, which combined elements of democracy, aristocracy, and monarchy. It was also notable for its religious tolerance, with Jews, Orthodox Christians, and Protestants all able to practice their faiths freely.

PaRTiTioNS oF PoLaND

The period between 1772 and 1918 in the history of Poland was characterized by a series of partitions, uprisings, and political transformations that shaped the country's identity and national consciousness. This period marked a time of great political, social, and economic upheaval, and the struggles of the Polish people to reclaim their independence from foreign powers became a defining feature of this era.

In 1772, Poland had been weakened by a series of internal conflicts and external pressures, and neighboring powers saw an opportunity to seize parts of its territory. Russia, Prussia, and Austria agreed to partition Poland, and by 1795, the country was divided among the three powers, effectively ending Poland's sovereignty. This period of foreign domination, known as the "Partitions of Poland," lasted for over a century and had a profound impact on Polish society.

The first partition in 1772 saw the annexation of much of the eastern regions of Poland by Russia. The second partition, in 1793, resulted in the loss of most of the western regions to Prussia, and the third partition, in 1795, resulted in the complete disappearance of the Polish state as it was divided between the three powers.

The Partitions of Poland were met with widespread resistance from the Polish people, who.

saw them as an assault on their national identity and sovereignty. Throughout the 19th century, a series of uprisings and rebellions were launched in an attempt to regain Polish independence. The most notable of these uprisings was the November Uprising of 1830-1831, which was sparked by the imposition of Russian military conscription on Polish territory. Despite initial successes, the uprising was eventually crushed by Russian forces, and many of its leaders were executed or exiled.

The failure of the November Uprising led to a period of cultural and intellectual revitalization known as the "Great Emigration." Many Polish artists, writers, and intellectuals fled to Western Europe, where they continued to work for the restoration of Polish independence. Among the most prominent figures of the Great Emigration were Adam Mickiewicz, Juliusz Słowacki, and Zygmunt Krasiński, who are regarded as some of the greatest poets in Polish literature.

The mid-19th century also saw the emergence of a new generation of Polish nationalists who sought to unify the various regions of Poland and create a modern, democratic state. In 1863, a new uprising broke out, known as the January Uprising, which was inspired by the success of the Italian Risorgimento and the Hungarian Revolution of 1848. The uprising was again crushed by Russian forces, and its leaders were either executed or exiled.

Despite the failures of these uprisings, they

contributed to a growing sense of national identity and consciousness among the Polish people. This sentiment was further strengthened by the emergence of a new political movement known as "Positivism," which sought to promote modernization, industrialization, and social reform in Poland.

The late 19th and early 20th centuries saw the emergence of a new political landscape in Poland, as various political parties and factions began to compete for power and influence. One of the most prominent of these was the Polish Socialist Party, which advocated for the rights of workers and peasants and sought to build a democratic, socialist state in Poland

WORLD WAR 1 & 2
INDEPENDENCE & SOVIET RULE

The period between 1918 and 1990 in the history of Poland was characterized by a series of political upheavals, economic challenges, and social transformations. The emergence of an independent Polish state after over a century of foreign domination marked the beginning of a new era in Polish history, and the struggles of the Polish people to build a democratic, prosperous, and just society continued to shape the country's identity and national consciousness.

In 1918, after the end of World War I, Poland regained its independence, and a new democratic state was established. The Treaty of Versailles recognized Poland as a sovereign state and granted it significant territories in the east, including parts of Ukraine and Belarus. The new state faced numerous challenges, including territorial disputes, economic instability, and political polarization, but it also witnessed a period of cultural and intellectual flourishing, known as the "Polish Renaissance."

The interwar period was marked by a struggle between different political parties and factions, with the socialist and nationalist movements competing for influence. The Polish Socialist Party advocated for workers' rights and social justice, while the National Democrats emphasized Polish national identity and Catholic values. The Sanation movement, led by Józef Piłsudski, sought to modernize the country and establish a strong, centralized government.

In 1939, Poland was invaded by Nazi Germany, and the country was once again plunged into a period of foreign domination. The German occupation was characterized by mass deportations, forced labor, and genocide, as millions of Polish Jews, as well as non-Jewish Poles, were killed in concentration camps and ghettos. The Polish Resistance fought back against the occupiers, and the Warsaw Uprising of 1944, although unsuccessful, became a symbol of Polish resistance and resilience.

After the end of World War II, Poland became a communist state under Soviet influence. The communist government, led by Władysław Gomułka, sought to modernize the country and promote economic development, but it also imposed strict controls on political and civil liberties. The Stalinist period of the late 1940s and early 1950s was marked by political purges, show trials, and repression, as the regime sought to consolidate its power and eliminate opposition.

In 1956, after the death of Stalin and the rise of Nikita Khrushchev to power in the Soviet Union, Poland experienced a period of liberalization known as the "Polish October." Gomułka was reinstated as the First Secretary of the Communist Party, and the government promised greater political freedoms and economic reforms. However, the reforms were short-lived, and in 1968, the regime cracked down on dissidents and intellectuals, leading to a period of censorship and repression known as the "Anti-Zionist Campaign."

The 1970s saw a period of economic stagnation and social unrest, as the government struggled to address the country's growing economic problems and social inequalities. In 1976, protests erupted in the city of Radom, and the government responded with force, killing several protesters and arresting thousands of others. This incident, known as the "Radom massacre," further eroded public trust in the government and fueled opposition to the regime.

In 1980, a new social movement emerged in Poland, known as Solidarity. Led by Lech Wałęsa, a former shipyard worker, Solidarity became a powerful force for social and political change, advocating for workers' rights, civil liberties, and democratic reforms. The government initially tolerated the movement, but as it grew in strength and popularity, it faced increasing repression, including martial law, arrests, and censorship.

The year 1989 marked a turning point in the history of Poland, as the country underwent a series of political transformations that paved the way for the establishment of a democratic and market-oriented society. The fall of communism in Poland was part of a broader wave of political change that swept through Eastern Europe, leading to the collapse of the Soviet Union and the end of the Cold War.

The events of 1989 were set in motion by a series of economic and political crises that had plagued Poland for several years. The country was facing high inflation, food shortages, and growing social unrest, and the government's attempts to address these problems had only led to further discontent and opposition.

In April 1989, the government agreed to hold partially free elections, in which opposition candidates were allowed to participate. The elections, held in June, were a resounding success for the opposition, with the Solidarity movement winning a majority of seats in the Sejm, the lower house of the Polish parliament.

The victory of Solidarity marked the beginning of a new era in Polish politics, as the movement's leaders began to negotiate with the government for greater political freedoms and economic reforms. In August 1989, an agreement was reached between the government and the opposition, known as the Round Table Talks. The talks resulted in the establishment of a new government with a coalition of Solidarity and communist party members.

The new government implemented a series of reforms, including the legalization of independent trade unions, the abolition of censorship, and the decentralization of power. In December 1989, a new constitution was adopted, establishing Poland as a democratic republic. The events of 1989 had profound on Polish society, as the country emerged from decades of communist rule and began a new chapter in its history.

Since the fall of communism, Poland has undergone significant economic and political reforms, becoming a democratic country with a market-oriented economy. Poland joined the European Union in 2004 and has since become an important player in European politics and economics.

WARSAW & KRAKOW

From its origins as a small settlement on the banks of the Vistula River to its emergence as a vibrant and dynamic European capital, Warsaw has witnessed numerous wars, invasions, and revolutions that have left a lasting mark on its landscape and identity.

The origins of Warsaw can be traced back to the 13th century, when a small fortified settlement was established by the Duke of Mazovia. Over the following centuries, the settlement grew in size and importance, becoming a significant center of trade, culture, and politics in the region. In the 16th century, Warsaw became the capital of the Polish-Lithuanian Commonwealth, a powerful state that dominated Central Europe for over two centuries.

During the 17th and 18th centuries, Warsaw was repeatedly invaded and occupied by foreign powers, including Sweden, Russia, and Prussia. The city suffered significant damage during these conflicts, with much of its architectural and cultural heritage destroyed or damaged.

The 19th century saw a period of revival and revitalization in Warsaw, as the city underwent a major urban transformation. New streets, buildings, and public spaces were constructed, and the city's cultural and intellectual life flourished. However, this period of growth and development was cut short by the outbreak of World War I, which saw Warsaw occupied by German forces.

During World War II, Warsaw became a symbol of resistance and resilience, as the city was subjected to one of the most brutal and devastating sieges in modern history. In 1939, Warsaw was invaded by Nazi Germany, and the city's Jewish population was subjected to mass deportation and extermination. The Polish Resistance fought back against the occupiers, launching the Warsaw Uprising in 1944 in an attempt to liberate the city.

The Warsaw Uprising was a heroic but ultimately unsuccessful effort, as German forces, supported by heavy artillery and air power, crushed the rebellion and destroyed much of the city in the process. The scale of the destruction was immense, with over 85% of the city's buildings destroyed or damaged, and an estimated 200,000 civilians killed.

After the end of World War II, Warsaw was rebuilt from the rubble, with a massive reconstruction effort that aimed to restore the city's historic architecture and cultural heritage. The process of reconstruction was long and difficult, with many challenges and setbacks, but the city was eventually restored to its former glory, becoming a vibrant and dynamic center of culture, politics, and commerce.

In the postwar period, Warsaw underwent a major transformation, as the city became the capital of communist Poland. The city's urban landscape was reshaped, with new housing developments, public spaces, and cultural institutions constructed to reflect the ideals of the socialist state. However, the communist period was also marked by political repression, censorship, and economic stagnation, as the country struggled to adapt to the demands of a rapidly changing world.

The fall of communism in 1989 marked a new chapter in the history of Warsaw, as the city embraced the values of democracy, market-oriented economy, and cultural diversity. The city's transformation over the past three decades has been remarkable, with new neighborhoods, public spaces, and cultural institutions emerging to reflect the city's dynamic and cosmopolitan character.

Today, Warsaw is a vibrant and dynamic European capital, with a rich and diverse cultural heritage, a thriving economy, and a growing reputation as a center of innovation and creativity. Despite its troubled history, the city remains a symbol of resilience and hope, a testament to the enduring spirit of its people and the power of human creativity and determination.

Founded in the 7th century, Krakow has been a center of culture, politics, and religion in the region, and its historic center is recognized as a UNESCO World Heritage Site.

Krakow's early history is shrouded in legend and myth, but it is believed to have been founded by a legendary ruler named Krakus, who is said to have defeated a dragon that was terrorizing the area. By the 10th century, Krakow had become an important center of trade and culture, and it was the capital of the Polish Kingdom from the 11th to the 16th century.

During the medieval period, Krakow was a center of learning and culture, with numerous universities, churches, and cultural institutions. The city was also a hub of international trade, with merchants from across Europe flocking to its markets and fairs.

The 16th century saw a period of political and economic decline in Krakow, as the city was repeatedly invaded and occupied by foreign powers, including Sweden, Russia, and Austria. However, the city's cultural and intellectual life continued to thrive, and Krakow became a center of the Polish Enlightenment in the 18th century.

The 19th century saw a period of revival and renewal in Krakow, as the city underwent a major urban transformation. New streets, buildings, and public spaces were constructed, and the city's cultural and intellectual life flourished. However, this period of growth and development was cut short by the outbreak of World War I, which saw Krakow occupied by Austrian forces.

During World War II, Krakow suffered significant damage and loss of life, as Nazi Germany occupied the city and subjected its Jewish population to mass deportation and extermination. Despite the devastation, Krakow emerged from the war as one of the few major cities in Poland that was largely unscathed by the conflict.

After the end of World War II, Krakow became part of communist Poland, and the city underwent a major transformation under the socialist state. New housing developments, public spaces, and cultural institutions were constructed, and the city's economy was modernized and expanded. However, the communist period was also marked by political repression, censorship, and economic stagnation, as the country struggled to adapt to the demands of a rapidly changing world.

The fall of communism in 1989 marked a new chapter in the history of Krakow, as the city embraced the values of democracy, market-oriented economy, and cultural diversity. The city's transformation over the past three decades has been remarkable, with new neighborhoods, public spaces, and cultural institutions emerging to reflect the city's dynamic and cosmopolitan character.

Today, Krakow is a vibrant and dynamic European city, with a rich and diverse cultural heritage, a thriving economy, and a growing reputation as a center of innovation and creativity. The city's historic center is filled with stunning architecture, museums, and cultural institutions, and the surrounding region is home to numerous natural and cultural attractions.

Despite its troubled history, Krakow remains a symbol of resilience and hope, a testament to the enduring spirit of its people and the power of human creativity and determination. The city's unique blend of history, culture, and beauty make it one of the most fascinating and enchanting cities in Europe.

Jasna Góra Monastery & Auschwitz - Birkenau

Jasna Góra Monastery is a Catholic pilgrimage site located in Częstochowa, Poland. It is famous for its Black Madonna icon, which is said to have miraculous powers. The monastery has a rich history that spans over 600 years.

The origins of the monastery can be traced back to the 14th century when a group of Pauline monks arrived in Częstochowa. They were invited by Prince Władysław Opolczyk to establish a monastery on the site of an old castle. The monks built a small chapel and began to live a life of prayer and contemplation.

In 1382, the monastery was attacked by the Hussites, a heretical group that had split from the Catholic Church. The monks were able to defend themselves and the monastery, and their victory was attributed to the intercession of the Virgin Mary.

Over the centuries, the monastery grew in size and importance. It became a center of pilgrimage for Catholics from all over Poland and beyond. In the 17th century, it was rebuilt in the Baroque style, with magnificent frescoes and sculptures added to the chapel.

In 1655, during the Swedish invasion of Poland, the monastery was besieged by the Swedish army. The monks and their supporters were able to hold out for over a month, despite being vastly outnumbered. Once again, their victory was attributed to the intercession of the Virgin Mary.

In the 18th century, the monastery became a center of cultural and intellectual activity. Many prominent figures, including poets, writers, and musicians, visited the monastery and contributed to its artistic and spiritual heritage. In the 19th century, the monastery played an important role in the struggle for Polish independence. The Black Madonna became a symbol of Polish resistance to foreign rule, and the monastery became a center of patriotic sentiment.

During World War II, the monastery was occupied by the German army. The Black Madonna was hidden by the monks, who were able to preserve it from destruction. After the war, the monastery was restored and became an important site of pilgrimage and devotion once again.

Today, Jasna Góra Monastery is one of the most important Catholic pilgrimage sites in the world. It attracts millions of visitors every year, who come to pray before the Black Madonna and to experience the spiritual and cultural richness of the site.

The Black Madonna is the centerpiece of the monastery's devotion. The icon is said to have miraculous powers and to have performed many.

miracles over the centuries. It is also a symbol of the Virgin Mary's protection of Poland and of the Polish people's devotion to her.

In addition to the Black Madonna, the monastery is home to many other treasures of art and culture. Its Baroque chapel is a masterpiece of Polish art, with magnificent frescoes and sculptures that depict scenes from the life of Christ and the Virgin Mary. The monastery also has a rich library and archive, which contains many valuable manuscripts and documents from Poland's history.

Jasna Góra Monastery has played an important role in the spiritual, cultural, and political life of Poland, and it continues to be a center of pilgrimage and devotion for Catholics from all over the world. Its Black Madonna icon is a symbol of the Virgin Mary's protection of Poland and of the Polish people's deep devotion to her. The monastery is a true treasure of art, culture, and spirituality, and it is a testament to the enduring power of faith and devotion.

The Auschwitz concentration camp, also known as Auschwitz-Birkenau, was a complex of Nazi concentration and extermination camps located in the Polish town of Oswiecim, about 37 miles west of Krakow. It is estimated that between 1.1 million and 1.5 million people, the vast majority of them Jews, were murdered at Auschwitz between 1940 and 1945. The history of Auschwitz is a sobering reminder of the atrocities committed during the

Holocaust and the depths of human cruelty.

Auschwitz was established in 1940 after the German occupation of Poland. The original camp, Auschwitz I, was built on the site of a former Polish army barracks. It was initially intended as a detention center for Polish political prisoners, but it quickly became a site for the imprisonment and extermination of Jews, Roma, and other groups considered undesirable by the Nazis.

Auschwitz II, also known as Auschwitz-Birkenau, was built in 1941 as a larger camp for the mass extermination of Jews. Birkenau had a capacity of 100,000 prisoners, and it was here that the Nazis built the infamous gas chambers and crematoria that were used to murder Jews and others by the millions. Auschwitz III, also known as Monowitz, was built in 1942 as a forced labor camp for the German chemical company IG Farben. Prisoners at Monowitz were forced to work in factories and mines, often in hazardous conditions, producing synthetic rubber and other materials for the German war effort.

Conditions in Auschwitz were brutal and inhumane. Prisoners were subjected to forced labor, starvation, disease, and torture. Medical experiments were also conducted on prisoners, including sterilization, genetic testing, and the testing of new drugs and treatments. Many prisoners were executed by firing squad, while others were sent to the gas chambers and crematoria.

Despite the horrific conditions at Auschwitz, there were acts of heroism and resistance among the prisoners. Prisoners organized clandestine education and cultural programs, and some attempted to escape or sabotage the camp's operations. The most famous act of resistance at Auschwitz was the revolt of the Sonderkommando, a group of Jewish prisoners who were forced to work in the gas chambers and crematoria. In October 1944, the Sonderkommando staged a revolt, using smuggled weapons to attack their guards and blow up one of the crematoria. The rebellion was ultimately crushed, and most of the Sonderkommando were executed, but it remains a symbol of the courage and determination of the prisoners at Auschwitz.

As the war drew to a close, the Nazis attempted to cover up the evidence of their crimes at Auschwitz. In January 1945, as Soviet forces approached, they began to evacuate the camp, forcing prisoners on death marches to other camps in Germany. Thousands died on these marches, and those who survived were subjected to further brutality in the camps they were sent to.

Auschwitz was liberated by Soviet forces on January 27, 1945. They found about 7,000 prisoners still alive, many of them sick and dying. The liberation of Auschwitz was a turning point in the war and a shocking revelation of the horrors of the Holocaust. The survivors of Auschwitz, along with other victims of the Nazi genocide, have since become a symbol of resilience and hope in the face of unimaginable suffering.

After the war, Auschwitz became a symbol of the Holocaust and a site of remembrance and mourning. The camp was preserved as a museum and memorial, and it has become one of the most visited sites of the Holocaust. The museum contains exhibits on the history of Auschwitz and the Holocaust, as well as artifacts, photographs, and personal belongings of the prisoners.

WiELiCZKa SaLT MiHE & MaLBoRK CaSTLE

The Wieliczka Salt Mine is one of the most fascinating and historically significant tourist attractions in Poland. Located in the town of Wieliczka, just 14 kilometers southeast of Krakow, the mine is a unique underground complex that spans over 287 kilometers and reaches a depth of 327 meters.

The salt mine has been in operation since the 13th century and was one of the largest producers of salt in Europe. Over the centuries, miners carved out intricate chambers and tunnels in the salt rock, creating a vast underground city that includes chapels, statues, and even an underground lake.

Visitors to the Wieliczka Salt Mine can take guided tours through the tunnels and see the incredible salt sculptures and carvings that line the walls. Some of the most impressive sights include the Chapel of St. Kinga, a beautiful underground chapel with walls, floors, and chandeliers all made entirely of salt, and the underground lake, which is filled with crystal-clear saltwater.

The Wieliczka Salt Mine is not just a testament to the ingenuity of medieval miners. It is also an important historical site that played a significant role in the economic and cultural development of the region. The mine was one of the main sources of wealth for the Polish Kingdom and was a hub of activity for centuries, attracting artisans, musicians, and other skilled workers to the area.

The mine also has a rich cultural history. During World War II, the Nazis used the mine as a storage facility for stolen artwork and other treasures. The Polish resistance even staged a successful operation to steal back the treasures, including the famous painting "Lady with an Ermine" by Leonardo da Vinci. Today, the Wieliczka Salt Mine is a popular destination for tourists from around the world. The mine attracts more than one million visitors each year, making it one of the most visited locations in Poland. The mine has also been designated a UNESCO World Heritage Site, recognizing its cultural and historical significance.

Visitors to the Wieliczka Salt Mine can choose from a variety of tours, ranging from basic guided tours to more extensive explorations of the underground chambers and tunnels. The mine is also a popular destination for weddings and other events, with the unique atmosphere and stunning architecture providing a memorable backdrop for any occasion. The Wieliczka Salt Mine is a true wonder of the world, showcasing the ingenuity and creativity of medieval miners and serving as a testament to the rich cultural and economic history of Poland. Whether you are a history buff, an art lover, or just looking for a unique adventure, a visit to the Wieliczka Salt Mine is an experience you will never forget.

Malbork Castle, also known as the Castle of the Teutonic Order in Malbork, is a massive fortress located in the town of Malbork in northern Poland. It is one of the largest castles in the world and has a rich history dating back to the 13th century.

The castle was initially built by the Teutonic Knights, a medieval Catholic military order, in the mid-13th century as a defensive stronghold against the pagan Prussians. The Teutonic Knights were a powerful force in Europe at the time and were responsible for numerous military campaigns in the Baltic region.

The original castle was constructed out of wood, but in the early 14th century, the Grand Master of the Teutonic Knights, Heinrich von Plauen, ordered the construction of a new castle made of brick. This new castle was designed to be a grand fortress that could house the knights and their army, as well as serve as the headquarters of the order.

Over the centuries, Malbork Castle was expanded and renovated multiple times, becoming more and more grand with each addition. The castle's walls were strengthened, and new towers were added, including the iconic Tower of the High Gate, which still stands today as the main entrance to the castle.

One of the most significant events in the castle's history occurred in the late 14th century when the Teutonic Knights were defeated by the Polish-Lithuanian forces at the Battle of Grunwald. This defeat marked the beginning of the decline of the Teutonic Knights, and their power in Europe began to wane.

In the 15th and 16th centuries, Malbork Castle served as the residence of the Polish kings and was renovated to reflect the Renaissance style of the time. The castle's chapel, which had been built in the Gothic style, was expanded and decorated with beautiful frescoes and stained glass. During the Second World War, the castle was heavily damaged by Allied bombing, and much of its interior was destroyed. After the war, the castle was painstakingly restored to its former glory, with much of the original Gothic and Renaissance architecture and decoration being recreated.

Today, Malbork Castle is a popular tourist destination, attracting visitors from all over the world who come to see the impressive fortress and learn about its rich history. The castle is now a UNESCO World Heritage site, and its museum contains a vast collection of medieval and Renaissance art, as well as artifacts related to the Teutonic Knights and the castle's long history. Malbork Castle is a magnificent fortress with a long and fascinating history. From its origins as a wooden fortification to its current status as a UNESCO World Heritage site, the castle has played an essential role in the history of Poland and Europe as a whole. Its impressive architecture and stunning interiors are a testament to the skill and creativity of the craftsmen who built it, and it remains one of the most impressive castles in the world today.

POLIN, WARSAW, & CZARTORYSKI MUSEUMS

The POLIN Museum of the History of Polish Jews is a world-class museum located in Warsaw, Poland. It is dedicated to preserving and showcasing the rich and diverse history of Jewish life in Poland, from the early days of Jewish settlement to the present. The museum is located in the heart of the former Jewish ghetto in Warsaw, which was one of the largest and most significant ghettos established by the Nazis during World War II.

The museum was opened in 2013, after more than a decade of planning and construction. Its name, POLIN, is derived from the Hebrew word for Poland, which means "rest here." The museum's mission is to educate visitors about the long and complex history of Polish Jewry, to promote intercultural understanding and dialogue, and to serve as a bridge between the past and present.

The museum's building is a stunning architectural achievement, designed by Finnish architect Rainer Mahlamäki and Polish architect Ilkka Länkinen. The museum's exterior is covered in glass panels, which are meant to symbolize the fractured and fragmented history of Polish Jewry. The interior of the museum is equally impressive, featuring interactive exhibits, multimedia displays, and a state-of-the-art theater.

The museum's permanent exhibition is divided into eight galleries, each of which focuses on a different period in Polish Jewish history. The galleries are arranged chronologically, beginning with the arrival of Jews in Poland in the Middle Ages and ending with the present day. The exhibits are designed to be engaging and immersive, with multimedia displays, interactive exhibits, and life-size recreations of historical scenes.

One of the highlights of the museum is the recreated Jewish street, which is designed to resemble the bustling streets of pre-war Jewish neighborhoods in Poland. Visitors can explore the shops, synagogues, and homes of the Jewish community, and learn about the daily life and traditions of Polish Jews. Another noteworthy exhibit is the Monumental Paintings Gallery, which features a series of large-scale paintings by the Polish-Jewish artist Samuel Hirszenberg. The paintings depict scenes from Jewish life in Poland, including weddings, funerals, and religious ceremonies, and provide a vivid and evocative glimpse into the world of Polish Jewry before World War II.

The POLIN Museum is a must-see destination for anyone interested in Jewish history, European history, or the intersection of the two. It is a powerful and moving tribute to the resilience, creativity, and diversity of the Jewish community in Poland, and a testament to the importance of remembering and learning from the past.

The Warsaw National Museum is a cultural institution located in the capital city of Poland, Warsaw. It was established in 1862 and is one of the oldest and largest museums in the country. The museum's collection includes over 800,000 exhibits of Polish and international art, including paintings, sculptures, drawings, and decorative art. The museum's primary mission is to preserve, study, and promote Polish culture and heritage.

The building that houses the museum is a remarkable architectural structure in itself. The main entrance is adorned with a monumental staircase and two allegorical figures of Art and Science. The museum's exhibition halls are divided into various sections that showcase different aspects of Polish art and history. Visitors can explore the collections of medieval and Renaissance art, 18th-century art, modern and contemporary art, decorative arts, and the history of Polish culture.

One of the most significant parts of the Warsaw National Museum is its collection of Polish paintings. The museum has an extensive collection of Polish art from the 19th and 20th centuries, including works by famous Polish artists such as Jozef Chelmonski, Julian Falat, Jacek Malczewski, and Tadeusz Makowski. The museum's collection also includes international art, such as works by Rembrandt, Rubens, and Rodin.

In addition to its impressive art collection, the museum also has a significant collection of historical artifacts that tell the story of Poland's past. The museum's historical collections include exhibits from various periods of Polish history, including the Middle Ages, the Renaissance, and the Baroque period. Visitors can see ancient weapons, armor, and other artifacts that give a glimpse into the lives of the people who lived in Poland in past centuries.

The museum's temporary exhibitions are also a must-see for visitors. These exhibitions showcase works by contemporary artists from Poland and other parts of the world. They provide an opportunity to learn about the latest trends and developments in art and culture.

The Warsaw National Museum is an essential part of Polish culture and heritage. It serves as a repository of the country's history and a platform for promoting Polish art and culture to the world. The museum's extensive collections and exhibitions attract visitors from all over the world and contribute to the promotion of cultural exchange between different countries. The Warsaw National museum's impressive collections and exhibitions provide a fascinating insight into the country's past and present. Visitors can spend hours exploring the various galleries and exhibitions and leave with a deeper appreciation for Polish art and culture.

The Czartoryski Museum is a grand and imposing museum situated in the heart of Krakow, Poland. It is known for its exquisite collection of art, antiques, and historical artifacts, making it one of the most significant cultural institutions in the city. The museum's history dates back to the late 18th century when Princess Izabela Czartoryska founded it as a way to preserve her family's vast collection of art and objects.

The museum's grand facade features intricate architectural details that reflect the building's rich history. Its grand entrance is adorned with tall columns, grand arches, and a series of decorative friezes that add to the building's grandeur. Upon entering, visitors are immediately struck by the museum's grandeur and sophistication. The interior is richly decorated, with grand halls and rooms adorned with ornate stucco, frescoes, and paintings.

The museum's collection is extensive, with artifacts and objects from various historical periods, including the Middle Ages, Renaissance, Baroque, and Enlightenment. Visitors can explore the museum's vast collection of European art, including masterpieces by famous artists such as Rembrandt, Botticelli, and Raphael. The collection also features a wide array of decorative arts, including exquisite ceramics, glassware, and silverware, as well as ancient weapons, armor, and tapestries.

One of the most popular exhibits at the Czartoryski Museum is the "Lady with an Ermine" painting by Leonardo da Vinci. This iconic masterpiece features a young woman holding a white ermine, and it is considered one of the artist's most significant works. Visitors can also view other works such as "Portrait of a Young Man" by Sandro Botticelli and "Portrait of a Lady with a Unicorn" by Raphael.

Apart from the art and historical artifacts, the museum's library is also a significant attraction. It contains over 250,000 volumes, including rare manuscripts, first editions, and ancient texts. The library is considered one of the most extensive collections of books and manuscripts in Poland.

The Czartoryski Museum is an excellent destination for art lovers, history enthusiasts, and anyone interested in exploring the rich cultural heritage of Poland. With its extensive collection of art and artifacts, as well as its stunning architecture and grand interiors, the museum offers a fascinating insight into the history and culture of Europe.

POLISH FOODS

Poland is a country with a rich culinary heritage and a variety of traditional dishes that are beloved by its people. Polish cuisine is known for its hearty and flavorful dishes, which are often influenced by neighboring countries such as Germany, Russia, and Ukraine. In this article, we will explore some of Poland's favorite foods, their origins, and how they are prepared.

Pierogi are one of Poland's most famous dishes and are enjoyed throughout the country. These are small dumplings that can be filled with a variety of ingredients, such as meat, cheese, sauerkraut, or fruit. Pierogi are typically boiled and then served with a variety of toppings, such as fried onions or sour cream. They are a staple at traditional Polish weddings and holiday celebrations.

Bigos is a hearty stew that is considered one of Poland's national dishes. It is made with sauerkraut, meat (usually beef or pork), and a variety of spices, including bay leaves, allspice, and juniper berries. The dish is typically simmered for several hours, allowing the flavors to meld together. Some versions of bigos also include smoked sausage or mushrooms.

Kielbasa is a type of sausage that is popular throughout Poland. There are many different varieties of kielbasa, each with its own unique flavor and texture. Some types of kielbasa are smoked, while others are boiled or grilled. Kielbasa is often served as a main dish, but it can also be used as an ingredient in other dishes, such as soups and stews.

Zapiekanka is a popular street food in Poland similar to a pizza. It consists of a long baguette that is sliced in half and then topped with a variety of ingredients, such as mushrooms, cheese, and onions. The zapiekanka is then baked in the oven until the cheese is melted and bubbly. Zapiekanka is a cheap and filling snack that is enjoyed by people of all ages.

Rosol is a traditional Polish soup that is made from chicken or beef broth, vegetables, and herbs. The soup is typically served with noodles or dumplings and is considered a comfort food in Poland. Rosol is often used as a remedy for colds and flu, as it is believed to have healing properties.

Sernik, or Polish cheesecake, is a beloved dessert in Poland. It is made with a mixture of cream cheese, eggs, sugar, and vanilla, and is typically baked in a crust made from crushed cookies or crackers. Sernik can be topped with a variety of ingredients, such as fruit or chocolate, and is often served with a dollop of whipped cream.

Paczki are traditional Polish doughnuts that are typically eaten on Fat Thursday, which falls on the Thursday before Lent. The doughnuts are filled with jam or custard and are deep-fried until they are golden brown. Paczki are a decadent treat that is enjoyed by people of all ages.

POLISH SPORTS

Poland has a strong sporting culture, with many popular sports enjoyed by people of all ages and backgrounds. From football to volleyball, athletics to skiing, Poland has a diverse range of sports and athletes who are celebrated for their achievements. In this essay, we will explore some of the most popular sports in Poland.

Football, or soccer as it is known in some countries, is by far the most popular sport in Poland. The country has a long and proud footballing tradition, with some of the best players in the world having come from Poland, including Robert Lewandowski, one of the top goal scorers in the world. The Polish national team has also achieved some impressive results, reaching the quarter-finals of the World Cup twice in their history. The top professional league in Poland is called Ekstraklasa, and it attracts large crowds and high levels of media attention.

Volleyball is another popular sport in Poland, with a strong tradition of success at the international level. The Polish men's volleyball team has won multiple Olympic medals and World Championships, and the women's team has also enjoyed success on the world stage. The Polish professional league, known as PlusLiga, is widely regarded as one of the best in the world, attracting top players from around the globe.

Basketball is also a popular sport in Poland, with a professional league known as the Polish Basketball League (PLK). Although the country has not yet enjoyed major international success in basketball, the sport has a dedicated following and is played at both the amateur and professional levels.

Track and field is another sport that enjoys a strong following in Poland. The country has produced some world-class athletes in disciplines such as sprinting, middle-distance running, and long-distance running. The annual Kamila Skolimowska Memorial, named after the Olympic gold medalist and world champion, is one of the most prestigious athletics events in Poland.

Skiing is a popular winter sport in Poland, with the Tatra Mountains providing a picturesque backdrop for skiing and snowboarding enthusiasts. The country has a number of ski resorts that attract tourists from around the world, and Polish skiers have achieved success at the Olympic and World Championship levels.

Other popular sports in Poland include handball, boxing, and ice hockey. Handball enjoys a large following, with the Polish national team having won multiple European Championships and the men's team having finished second in the World Championships. Boxing has produced a number of successful fighters, including Tomasz Adamek, who held world titles in two different weight classes. Ice hockey is also popular, with a professional league known as the Polska Hokej Liga (PHL) and the national team having competed in multiple World Championships and Olympic Games.

Poland has a diverse range of popular sports, with football, volleyball, basketball, athletics, and skiing being among the most widely enjoyed. The country has produced many world-class athletes, and its sports culture is an important part of its national identity.

WELCOME TO POLAND!

CHECK OUT OUR OTHER BOOKS!

TEACHING KIDS AROUND THE WORLD!

FOLLOW KID HISTORY!

  @KIDHISTORYBOOKS

amazon.com/author/loganstover

ABOUT KID HISTORY!

"LOGAN HAS A GIFT FOR TEACHING HISTORY TO ALL AGES. HE MAKES LEARNING HISTORY FUN!"

LOGAN STOVER IS AN EDUCATOR, FILMMAKER, & THE CREATOR OF KID HISTORY CHILDREN'S BOOKS!

@LEARN.WITH.LOGAN

amazon.com/author/loganstover

Made in the USA
Middletown, DE
28 September 2024